The Chesapeake
The Coastal Defenses of the Chesapeake Bay During World War Two

By Terrance McGovern

Proof firing of a 16-inch gun at Battery Ketcham (#120) at Fort Story, VA (October 1942 – Casemate Museum Collection)

Previously published in FORT: The International Journal of Fortifications and Military Architecture
The annual publication of the Fortress Study Group

Three Sisters Press
A Division of McGovern Publishing

Distributed by
Pictorial Histories Publishing Company

Copyright @ 2010 by Terrance McGovern

Photographs are identified in the captions as to source. All photographs are copyrighted by the source, unless the source is the U.S. Government, in which case these photographs are in the public domain.
All rights reserved in all media worldwide. No part of the book may be used or reproduced without written permission of the author.

Library of Congress Control Number: 2010929891
ISBN 978-1-57510-149-1

First Printing: June 2010
Layout by Stephen Dent (sfdent@dircon.co.uk)
Printing by John Davis (jdavis@icfi.com)

Three Sisters Press
1700 Oak Lane
McLean, VA 22101 USA

Acknowledgements

Preparing the story of defenses of the Chesapeake Bay during World War II was only possible through the work of many Coast Defense Study Group (CDSG) members who have researched the U.S. National Archives and U.S. Army records for many years to yield the details about these defenses. This book would not have been written without this collective effort. I am particularly indebted to Mark Berhow, Bolling Smith, Fielding Tyler, Dick Weinert, Glen Williford, and Robert Zink for their advice and for providing documents and photographs for this work. I would also like to express my appreciation for those in Tidewater area who made my many trips there so enjoyable and allowed me access to many of the sites discussed in this book. I am also indebted to Dave Bassett, Terry Gander, and Stephen Dent for their efforts to edit and publish this work for the first time in Fortress Study Group's journal FORT 2008. Thanks also to Geoff Dennison for additional technical help. I want to thank my wife, Margaret Hogan, for allowing me the time to visit the many sites and to write the book. Finally, I want to congratulate my three daughters (Rebecca, Rachel, & Alana) for taking on the challenge to publish and sell this book to the general public.

Please direct your comments or corrections to the author at 1700 Oak Lane, McLean, VA 22101 USA or tcmcgovern@att.net. Please visit the web for other coast defense books from **Redoubt Press**, a division of McGovern Publishing.

Front Cover Photo: *Drill on a 16-inch howitzer at Battery Pennington, Fort Story, VA.* (1941- Still Pictures Collection, NARA)

Back Cover Photos: (1) *Gun drill on 8-inch Model 1888 M1A1 on a Model 1918 railway carriage at Fort Monroe, VA.* (1943 – Casemate Museum Collection); **(2)** *Planting mines from US Army Mine Planter* General Schofield *and Army Mine Yawl L66 in Chesapeake Bay.* (May 1942 – Still Pictures Collection, NARA); **(3)** *Practice 16-inch shell with messages at Battery Pennington, Fort Story, VA.* (1942 – Casemate Museum Collection); **(4)** *The SS* Tiger *after being torpedoed by a German U-Boat off the entrance to the Chesapeake Bay in 1942.* (1942 – Casemate Museum Collection); **(5)** *Gun drill on a 155-mm Model 1917/18 GPF gun on a 180-degree Panama Mount at Fort Story, VA.* (1942 – Casemate Museum Collection)

Pictorial Histories Publishing Company
713 South Third Street West
Missoula, Montana 59801
406/549-8488
406/729-9280
www.pictorialhistoriespublishing.com

The Coastal Defenses of Chesapeake Bay During World War Two

Terrance McGovern

The defense of America's seacoast has been one of the key concerns of United States' military policy since the earliest years of the Republic. American coast defense steadily evolved through the age of muzzle loading cannon, ever larger breech loading weapons, and finally to the culmination in large, long range guns capable of targeting the largest and most heavily armed warships of their age. By the end of World War II, the United States had some of the strongest coastal defenses in the world. Given the importance of the US naval bases around Norfolk, Virginia and the shipyards of Hampton Roads, the seacoast defenses protecting Chesapeake Bay contained the largest collection of firepower in the continental United States as they reached their apex during World War II.

Background

The defense of the lower Chesapeake Bay really began with the start of construction of Fort Monroe, Virginia, in 1819. Earlier fortifications were small and only able to offer limited protection to a very restricted area. Fort Monroe, located on Old Point Comfort at the tip of the Virginia Peninsula, was the largest masonry fort ever erected in the United States and effectively protected the important port of Hampton Roads and the immediate surrounding waters. Advances in military technology during the American Civil War made the stone and brick bastion fort obsolete and it was not until 1890 that modern defenses were begun. In 1886 the Board on Fortifications or Other Defenses, more familiarly known as the Endicott Board after its president, US Secretary of War William C

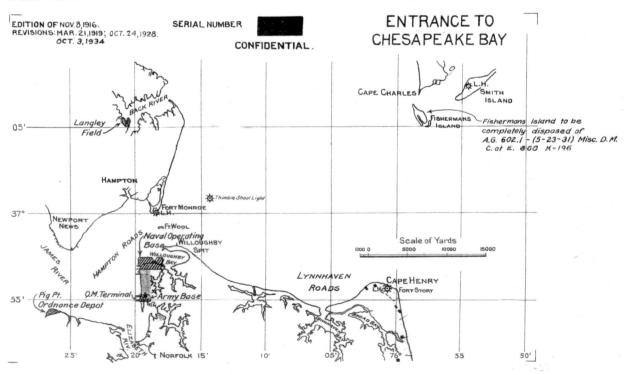

Plan for Entrance to Chesapeake Bay, VA. from Report of Completed Works – U.S. Corp of Engineers. (October 1934 – Textural Records Collection, NARA)

Model 1900 6-inch guns at target practice at Battery Montgomery, Fort Monroe, VA. (1941 – Casemate Museum Collection)

Target practice on the 12-inch disappearing guns of Fort Parrott, Fort Monroe, VA. (1930's – Casemate Museum Collection)

TABLE I
FORT MONROE

Battery name	# of guns	calibre	carriage type	service years	current status
Anderson	8	12"	M	1898-1943	
Ruggles	8	12"	M	1898-1943	
DeRussy	3	12"	DC	1904-1944	
Parrott	2	12"	DC	1906-1943	emplacements used for AMTB #23
Humphreys	1	10"	DC	1897-1910	destroyed
Eustis	2	10"	DC	1901-1942	destroyed
Church	2	10"	DC	1901-1942	
Bomford	2	10"	DC	1897-1940	destroyed
N.E. bastion	1	10"	DC	1900-1908	
Barber	1	8"	BC	1898-1915	destroyed
Parapet	4	8"	BC	1898-1915	mostly buried
Water	1	8"	BC	1897-1898	
Montgomery	2	6"	P	1904-1948	guns removed '20s, guns repl. '41, destroyed
Gatewood	4	4.7"	A	1898-1914	mostly buried
Irwin	4	3"	MP	1903-1922	all guns rem. '20s, 2-3" P. repl. '46

FORT WOOL

Battery name	# of guns	calibre	carriage type	service years	current status
Claiborne	2	6"	DC	1908-1918	
Dyer	2	6"	DC	1908-1917	
Gates	2	6"	DC	1908-1942	converted to BC#229 in 1944
Lee	4	3"	P	1905-1946	2 guns to Ft. J. Custis, 2 guns to Irwin, Ft. Monroe
Hindman	2	3"	P	1905-1946	

KEY: M – Mortar   DC – Disappearing   BC – Barbette   P – Pedestal   MP – Masking Parapet   A – Armstrong

Hampton Roads with Fort Monroe on Old Point Comfort in the foreground and Fort Wool on the Rip Raps in the center of the roads and Willoughby Spit in the background with the Norfolk Naval Operating base to the right. (June 6, 1927 – Still Pictures Collection, NARA)

Endicott, recommended the construction of detached batteries behind earthen parapets surmounting and protecting concrete magazines, bomb proofs, and storerooms. Armament was to consist of breech loading steel rifles and mortars in various sizes, mounted on disappearing carriages, barbette carriages, and turrets, and supported by minefields and torpedo boats. As a result of the Endicott program, between 1896 and 1906 the armament listed in Table I was installed at Fort Monroe and Fort Wool, a small supporting work built on an artificial island in the mouth of Hampton Roads.[1]

By the beginning of World War I much of this armament was obsolescent compared to the newer big gun dreadnoughts. Advances in naval fire control had made 14-inch and 15-inch gun battleships formidable antagonists for any fixed fortifications. The future site (343 acres) of Fort Story on Cape Henry was acquired in 1914 and in April 1917 temporary batteries mounting two 6-inch guns and two 5-inch guns were placed there, while Fisherman Island (225 acres), immediately off Cape Charles, had temporary batteries mounting four 5-inch guns which were installed in May 1917. For the first time, antiaircraft guns were installed at Fort Monroe, Newport News and Hopewell, Virginia; while in the bay anti-submarine nets were laid between Fort Monroe and Fort Wool, and another one in the vicinity of Thimble Shoals.

Despite these efforts, Chesapeake Bay remained for all purposes open sea because of the 20 mile width between the Capes. The entrance to the Chesapeake Bay always presented challenges to American military planners due its extreme width. Deepwater channels enter the bay on both the north and south, and there are no islands between these channels on which to place defenses to cover these shipping channels. Since it was impossible to defend the entire width of the entrance, harbor defenses were required at each individual port within the bay – Norfolk, Hampton, Washington, Baltimore, and Annapolis – since the colonial era. Advances in construction techniques allowed the Taft Board (a civilian-military committee charged with updating the Endicott Board report) in 1906 to offer a plan to close this body of water by the construction of an artificial island on the middle ground shoals to mount several coast artillery batteries. This island fort would be similar to those constructed by the Japanese in Tokyo Bay and would, in conjunction with forts on Cape Henry and Cape Charles, bar the entrance to the bay to warships. This plan was never selected due to lack of funding and concerns about the stability of such an island. Involved in a first actual effort to solve this problem were four 16-inch howitzers with a range of 24,540 yards that were emplaced between 1921 and 1922 at Battery Pennington, Fort Story. But no further armament followed immediately and the howitzers, mounted completely without protection on circular gun emplacements with dispersed cinder block magazines, offered only a partial and unsatisfactory solution to the problem. In theory, enemy capital ships needed to be kept some 35,000 yards from the mouth of the bay.[2]

Preparing for World War II

The basic mission of the Harbor Defenses of Chesapeake Bay were designed to ensure freedom of movement in and out of Chesapeake Bay by the US Navy as well as to deny an enemy access to the bay and to protect shipping and harbor facilities. The inner defenses at Fort Monroe and Fort Wool protected Hampton Roads and the inner harbor. The outer defenses at Cape Henry (Fort Story – named after MG John P. Storey in 1916) and Cape Charles (Fort John Custis – first named Fort Winslow after BG Eben E Winslow in 1941 but had its name changed in 1942 to honor a famous local hero, Captain John P. Custis) protected the mouth of the bay and the shipping channels to Washington and Baltimore.[3] The military reservation at Cape Charles was established in 1940 and would encompass 721 acres. It should be noted that no attempt was made to prevent landings at all points along the coast, but only to protect vital harbors.

The US War Department was well aware of the shortcomings of American coast artillery compared to modern

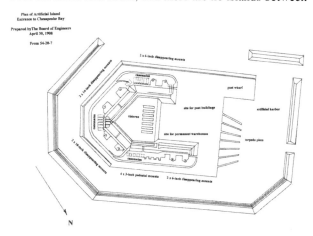

Proposed plan for a Chesapeake Bay Middle Ground fort on a artificial island in 1908. (Drawn from records at NARA by Glen Williford)

Old Point Comfort and Fort Monroe, VA. (December 18, 1935 – Still Pictures Collection, NARA)

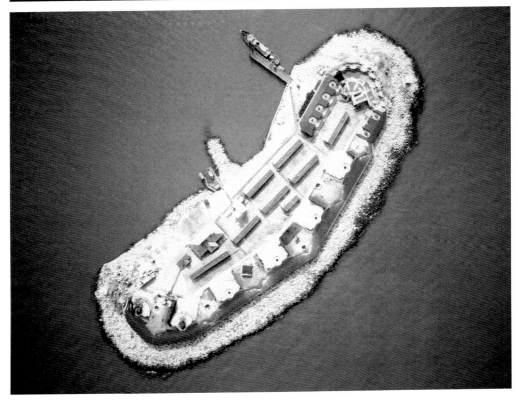

Battery Gates still has it 6-inch disappearing guns in this photo of Fort Wool, VA (1935 – Still Pictures Collection, NARA)

warships. During the early 1930s the US Army developed a long-range 16-inch barbette carriage gun as the standard weapon against capital ships. Little work, however, was actually done to improve the harbor defenses and only a few of these 16-inch batteries were constructed using a design similar to Battery Pennington. When the ultimate fate of the British and French fleets became a matter of concern in 1940, a complete reassessment of harbor defense was undertaken. In a report on July 27, 1940, the U.S Army Harbor Defense Board recommended the general adoption of the 16-inch gun as the primary weapon and the 6-inch gun as the secondary weapon in all fixed harbor defenses. Until the new gun batteries were completed, numbers of the older armament (disappearing guns and seacoast mortars) would be retained in service, along with widespread use of the World War I era 155m field gun to fill in the gap until the 6-inch batteries could be constructed. In September 1940, the US Secretary of War formally approved the modernisation programme.[4]

The emplacements for the new batteries would differ radically from previous designs, as protective defenses from both naval shelling and aerial bombing were now provided. The 16-inch guns were mounted in pairs inside

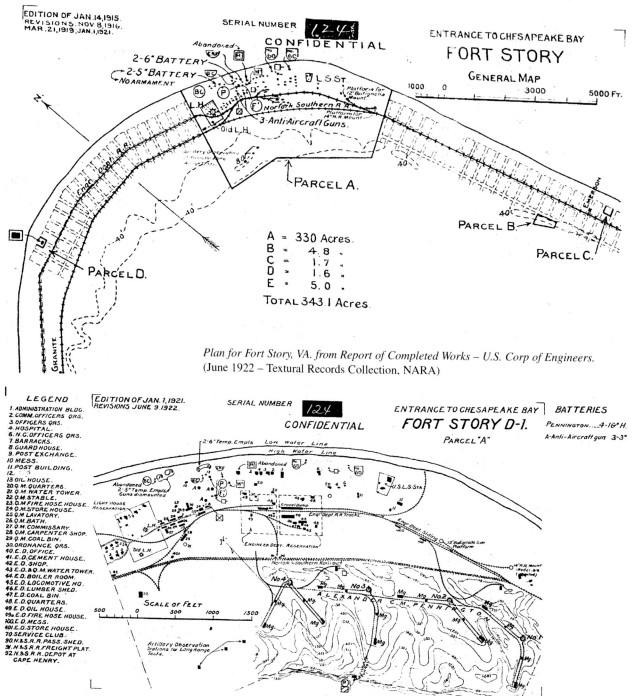

Plan for Fort Story, VA. from Report of Completed Works – U.S. Corp of Engineers. (June 1922 – Textural Records Collection, NARA)

Detailed plan for Fort Story, VA. from Report of Completed Works – U.S. Corp of Engineers. (June 1922 – Textural Records Collection, NARA)

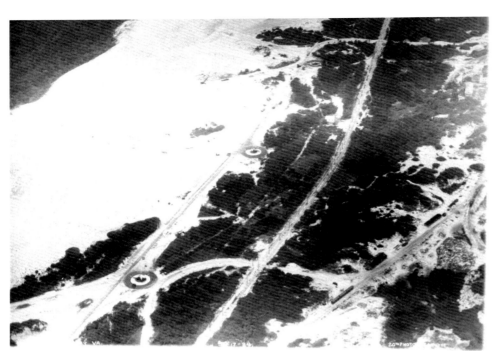

Three of the four 16-inch howitzers at Battery Pennington, Fort Story, VA (May 17, 1924 – Still Pictures Collection, NARA)

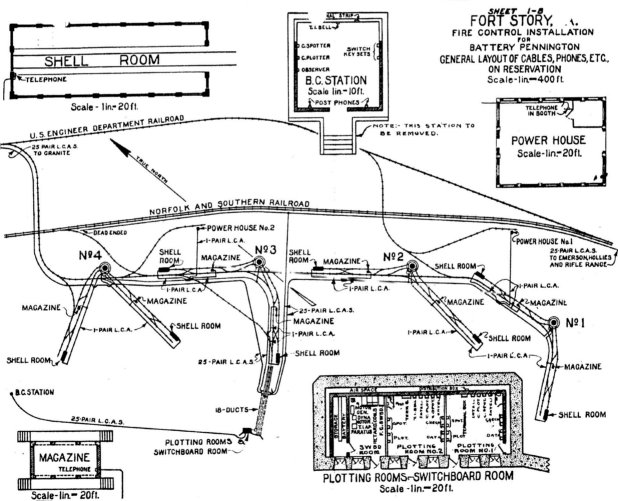

Report of Completed Works – U.S. Corp of Engineers plan for Battery Pennington, Fort Story, VA. (November 1924 – Textural Records Collection, NARA)

Terrance McGovern

Battery Pennington with three of its 16-inch howitzer in view at Fort Story, VA. (February 4, 1938 – Still Pictures Collection, NARA)

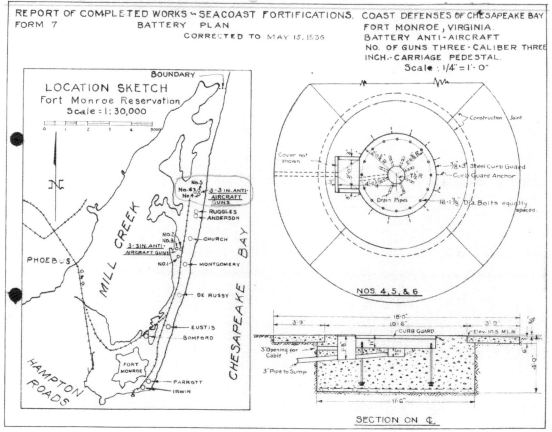

Report of Completed Works – U.S. Corp of Engineers plan for anti-aircraft battery, Fort Monroe, VA. (May 1936 – Textural Records Collection, NARA)

Cape Henry and its lighthouse at Fort Story, VA. (May 17, 1924 – Still Pictures Collection, NARA)

Cape Henry at Fort Story, VA. (May 17, 1924 – Still Pictures Collection, NARA)

One of the four 16-inch howitzers at Battery Pennington, Fort Story, VA (May 17, 1924 – Still Pictures Collection, NARA)

Battery Pennington with four 16-inch howitzers at Fort Story, VA (May 17, 1924 – Still Pictures Collection, NARA)

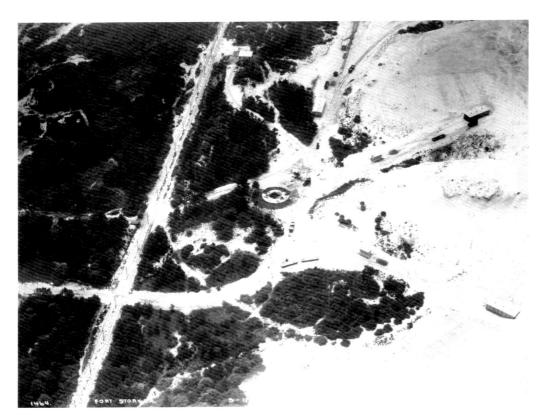

One of the four 16-inch howitzers at Battery Pennington, Fort Story, VA (May 17, 1924 – Still Pictures Collection, NARA)

8-inch railway guns firing in positions at Fort Monroe, VA (1940 – Casemate Museum Collection)

Firing drill on a 3-inch Model 1917 anti-aircraft gun at Anti-Aircraft Battery No. 2, Fort Monroe, VA. (1942 – Casemate Museum Collection)

thick concrete casemates approximately 500 feet apart. Between the casemates was a service tunnel off which extended a series of galleries which contained magazines, generators, and various storage and operating facilities. The entire structure was roofed by 8 to 10 feet of reinforced concrete, which in turn was covered with a layer of sand up to 20 feet thick. The guns in the casemates were further protected by armour shields and additional overhead concrete and steel. This standard design became known as the #100 Series Battery Construction. All the 16-inch guns used in the Chesapeake Bay defenses were US Navy guns manufactured in the 1920's which became available to the US Army as a result of the Washington Naval Conference of 1922 limitations on new warship building. This 16-inch gun had a range of 45,155 yards or about 25 miles. The new 6-inch guns had a thick wrap-around armor shield and they were mounted in pairs on open concrete pads. Between the gun positions was an

Workers make adjustments to a 6-inch Model 1905A2 gun on a shielded barbette carriage M1 at Battery #227 on Fisherman Island, VA. (1943 – Casemate Museum Collection)

Table II

Tactical #	Construction #	Armament. Location Status (December 1941)
1	120	Two 16-in. guns (Battery Ketcham), Ft. Story, under construction
2	–	Two 16-in. howitzers, Battery Pennington, Ft. Story, existing
3	–	Two 16-in. howitzers, Battery Walke, Ft. Story, existing
4	121	Two 16-in. guns, Ft. Story, authorized
5	225	Two 6-in. shielded barbette guns (Battery Cramer), Ft. Story, authorized
5T	–	Four 155-mm. GPF guns, Ft. Story, existing
6	224	Two 6-in. M1900 barbette guns (Battery Worcester), Ft. Story, existing
7	–	Mine Battery, Ft. Story Casemate, existing
8	–	Mine Battery, Fisherman Island Casemate, authorized
8	123	Two 16-in. guns, Cape Charles, authorized (later deleted in 1942)
9	228	Two 6-in. shielded guns, Cape Charles, authorized (not completed)
10	226	Two 6-in. shielded guns, Ft. Story, authorized
11	227	Two 6-in. shielded guns, Fisherman Island, authorized
12	122	Two 16-in. guns, (Battery Winslow) Cape Charles, under construction
13	229	Two 6-in. disappearing guns, Battery Gates, Ft. Wool, existing (to be replaced by shielded 6-inch guns on barbette mounts – not completed)
14	–	Two 3-in. guns, Battery Hindman, Ft. Wool, existing
15	–	Mine Battery, Ft. Monroe Casemate, existing
16	–	Four 3-in. guns, Battery Henry Lee, Ft. Wool, existing
17	–	Two 6-in. barbette guns, Battery Montgomery, Ft. Monroe
18	124	Two 16-in. guns, Ft. Monroe, authorized (later deleted in 1942)
AA No 1	–	Three 3-in. anti-aircraft guns, Ft. Story, existing
AA No 2	–	Three 3-in. anti-aircraft guns, Ft. Monroe, existing
AA No 3	–	Three 3-in. anti-aircraft guns, Ft. Monroe, existing
W	–	Four 155-mm GPF guns, Ft. Monroe, existing
Y	–	Two 8-in. railway guns, Ft. Story, existing
Z	–	Two 8-in. railway guns, Ft. Monroe, existing

earth covered reinforced concrete structure containing the magazines, generators, and storage and operating space. This standard design became known at the #200 Series Battery Construction. These guns had a range of 27,530 yards or about 15 miles.[5]

As a result of this modernisation program, the existing and proposed armament to defend Chesapeake Bay at the end of 1941 is shown in Table II.[6]

Sites for the construction of the new batteries were authorized by the US Secretary of War on November 27, 1940, and April 7, 1941, and the modernisation of Battery Gates on February 1, 1941. Work had already begun April 15, 1940, on Battery Construction No 224, subsequently designated Battery Worcester.[7] As a temporary measure, the emplacements for two 8-inch railway guns and 155-mm towed batteries had been approved on November 24, 1933, in case of emergency at Fort Story.

There were railway spurs and firing positions at Fort Monroe and Fort Story during and after World War I. Several types of railway units were assigned to these posts both on permanent and temporary basis using a range of weapons (8-inch guns, 12-inch mortars, and 12-inch guns). Effective fire control was an important aspect for the effective use of these batteries so a network of 90 fire control stations, primarily on about 35 steel towers rising from 90 feet to 145 feet were constructed along the coast for range about 20 miles to both the north and south of the entrance to the bay. Each tower contained several stations each on their own level and each assigned to a unique battery. These stations would contain azimuth instruments or depression position finders or both types of fire control instruments to target enemy ships and would pass these co-ordinates on to the plotting rooms at each battery via telephone. This network allowed the seacoast batteries to

52A. One of the two 6-inch Model 1905A2 gun on a shielded barbette carriage M1 at Battery #227 on Fisherman Island, VA. (1943 – Casemate Museum Collection)

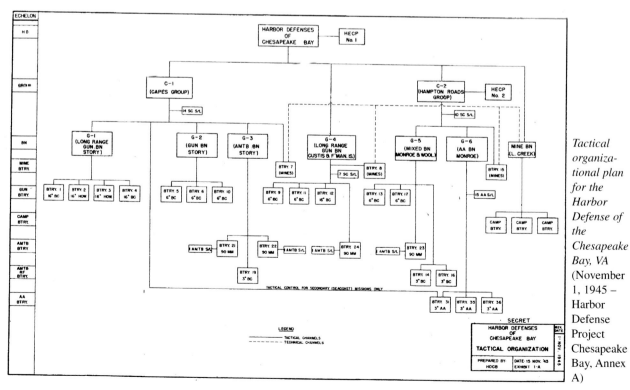

Tactical organizational plan for the Harbor Defense of the Chesapeake Bay, VA (November 1, 1945 – Harbor Defense Project Chesapeake Bay, Annex A)

Construction of Battery #227 on Fisherman Island, VA receives its sand protective covering. (1943 – Casemate Museum Collection)

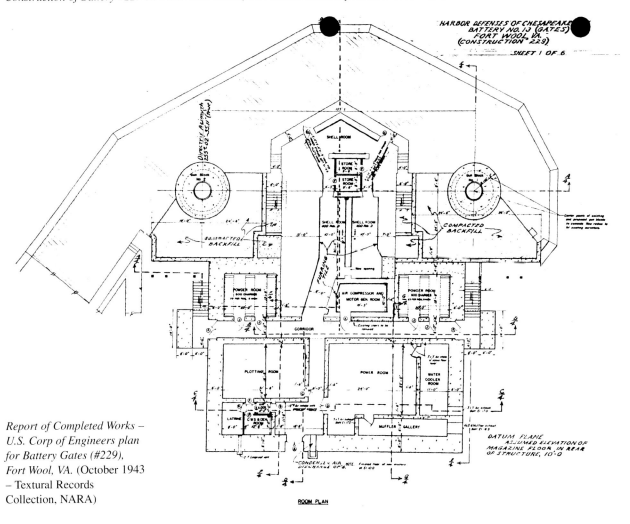

Report of Completed Works – U.S. Corp of Engineers plan for Battery Gates (#229), Fort Wool, VA. (October 1943 – Textural Records Collection, NARA)

fire at targets which could not be observed from the battery location. Also, assisting the fire control stations in targeting at night was a network of seacoast searchlights. These 60-inch lights were mounted in metal shelters on steel towers (20 to 50 feet high) with power generators in a separate structure and directed from controllers located away from the searchlight.

To command the defenses of Chesapeake Bay after World War I, the US Army had established the Coast Defenses of Chesapeake Bay on November 27, 1922, to include Forts Monroe, Wool, and Story. Re-designated the Harbor Defenses of Chesapeake Bay, this tactical command was part of the Third Coast Artillery District. Headquarters of both the district and harbor defenses was located at Fort Monroe. In November 1940 the district passed from the command of the Third Corps Area to First Army and the Northeast Defense Command. With the outbreak of war, the Third Coast Artillery District was re-designated the Chesapeake Bay Sector of the Eastern Defense Command on December 12, 1941, and headquarters of the Harbor Defenses of Chesapeake Bay moved to Fort Story. Brig. Gen. Rollin L. Tilton commanded the sector during its entire existence and the Harbor Defenses of Chesapeake Bay before the sector's activation and after its deactivation. The sector eventually grew to cover the coastal area from the Delaware-Maryland state line to the southern boundary of Onslow County, North Carolina, just above Wilmington. At its peak, there were over 15,000 troops assigned directly to the Chesapeake Bay Sector.[8]

While work began on the new batteries, several of the older guns were brought back in service for the first time in years. On June 10, 1941, the 16-inch howitzers at Fort Story fired their first service practice since 1928. This was followed on August 6, 1941, by the proof firing of the two 6-inch guns of Battery Worcester at Fort Story. This was the first battery of the new design constructed, but it still mounted the old Model 1900 6-inch guns on Model 1900 barbette carriages. The battery had been completed on

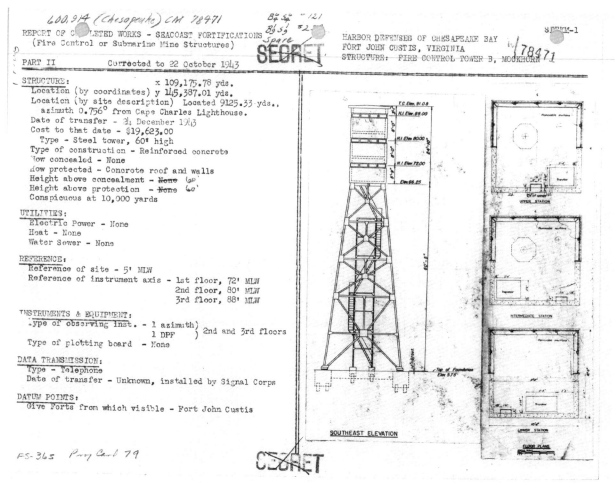

Report of Completed Works – U.S. Corp of Engineers for Fire Control Tower B at Mockhorn Island, VA. (October 1943 – Textural Records Collection, NARA)

Group fire control concrete tower at Fort John Custis, VA upon completion in 1942. April 1942 – Casemate Museum Collection)

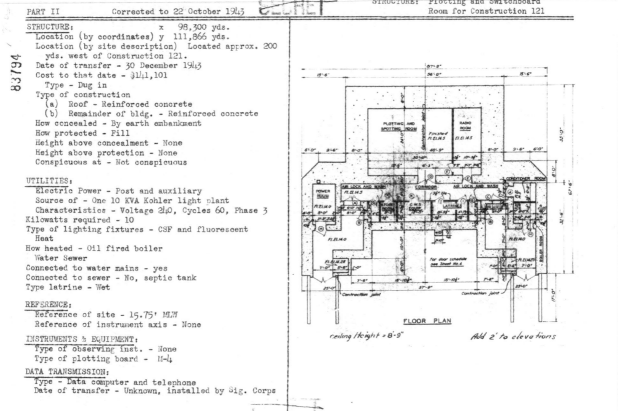

Report of Completed Works – U.S. Corp of Engineers for the protected and separate Plotting and Switchboard Room for Battery #121, Fort Story, VA. (October 1943 – Textural Records Collection, NARA)

April 1, 1941, at a cost of $76,237. This was followed by a target practice with the 6-inch disappearing guns of Battery Gates at Fort Wool, the first time these weapons had been fired since World War I. Work began on Battery Construction No 120 (Battery Ketcham), one of the new 16-inch batteries at Fort Story. On August 18, 1941, work was also started, on Battery Construction No 122 (Battery Winslow), two more 16-inch guns, on Cape Charles. In September 1941 it was arranged for the Pennsylvania Railroad to help construct the firing spurs for the temporary battery of 8-inch railway guns at Cape Charles.[9]

In addition to the extensive gun batteries, underwater defenses were also provided. In January 1941, a plan provided for an outer defense of 22 groups of controlled mines in two fields in two lines each in the main channel northeast of Cape Henry, and an inner defense of six groups in two lines in Chesapeake Bay near Thimble Shoal Light. There was also to be a US Navy mine field of contact mines between the northern tip of Cape Charles and the north edge of the main channel linking up with the controlled mine field. In addition, there was to be an anti-motor torpedo boat boom and submarine net obstructions in the channel southwest of Thimble Shoals and another from Fort Monroe to Willoughby Spit on the Norfolk side. Another net was included at the mouth of the York River. The Fifth Naval District had at the same time established the Inshore Patrol, with its command post at Fort Story. The US Navy had also laid hydrophones to seaward side of the minefields for the surveillance of the bay entrance at night or in conditions of poor visibility.

In December 1941, 140 acres of land for the Little Creek Mine Base was acquired from the Pennsylvania Railroad adjacent to the railroad ferry landing in Princess Anne County on the south shore of Chesapeake Bay. Construction of mine storage space, magazines, cable tanks, loading rooms, wharfs, boat repair facilities, barracks, and other buildings started immediately. US Army mine planters and mine laying batteries used this base for operations in the outer minefields.[10]

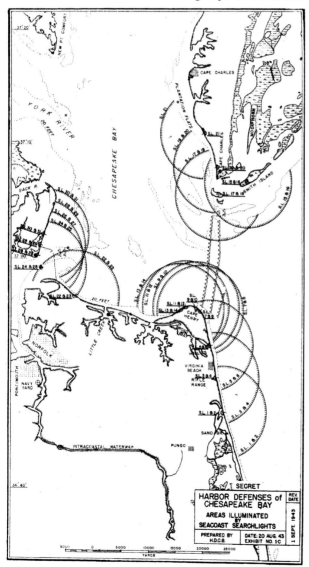

Plan of arc of illumination for seacoast searchlights in the Harbor Defense of the Chesapeake Bay, VA (September 1, 1943 – Harbor Defense Project Chesapeake Bay, Annex A)

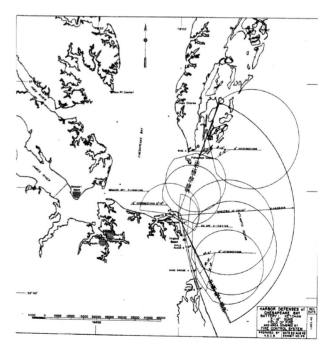

Plan of field of fire for Battery Ketcham (#120) and its seacoast fire control stations in the Harbor Defense of the Chesapeake Bay, VA (November 1, 1945 – Harbor Defense Project Chesapeake Bay, Annex A)

Battery Worcester (#224) and Fort Story, VA (September 17, 1941 – Still Pictures Collection, NARA)

Gun drill at the 6-inch Model 1900 gun at Battery Worcester, Fort Story, VA (1941 – Still Pictures Collection, NARA)

Drill on a 16-inch howitzer at Battery Pennington, Fort Story, VA. (1941 – Still Pictures Collection, NARA)

16-inch Model 1920 howitzer on Model 1920 barbette carriage at Battery Pennington, Fort Story, VA. (February 4, 1938 – Still Pictures Collection, NARA)

Surviving World War II barracks at Camp Pendleton, Virginia Beach (Photograph taken October 2000 – Source: McGovern Collection)

A rare surviving battery commander's station on a steel tower at Fort Wool. This station serves Battery Gates/#229. (October 2000 – McGovern Collection)

Fire Control Tower (completed in 1941) at Parcel C, Virginia Beach. This tower was removed in 2004. (October 2000 – McGovern Collection)

Gun casemate for Battery Winslow (BC#122) at Fort John Custis. (October 2000 – McGovern Collection)

Main service corridor for Battery Winslow (#122) at Fort John Custis This corridor connects the two gun casemates where the 16-inch guns were emplaced. The battery's power room, shell rooms, powder rooms and other storage areas are located off this corridor. (October 2000 – McGovern Collection)

A gun emplacement for a fixed 90-mm gun was built into Battery Parrott' disappearing gun loading platform during World War II of AMTB Battery #23. (October 2000 – McGovern Collection)

Two 3-inch rapid fire guns remain today at Battery Irwin, Fort Monroe. These M1903 guns were provided with new shields during World War Two when these guns were located at Fort Wool. (October 2000 – McGovern Collection)

Three surviving motor generators in the power room of Battery #227 on Fisherman Island. Only a few of these World War II batteries retain their machinery, most have been scrapped. (October 2000 – McGovern Collection)

Entrance to Fort Monroe's third mine casemate in the old casemates of the Third Front. During World War II this casemate was built with this concrete structure serving as a gas proof entrance. (October 2000 – McGovern Collection)

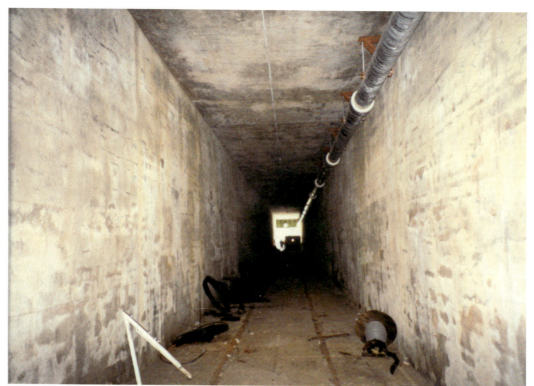

Inside the rail tunnel at Battery Pennington, Fort Story. This tunnel was constructed to provide access through the dunes from the main railway line to the battery's rail system. The tunnel also could be used to provide shelter for railway equipment. (October 2000 – McGovern Collection)

The old and new lighthouses at Cape Henry, Fort Story. Located under the old lighthouse's dune is the original mine casemate. (October 2000 – McGovern Collection)

Entrance to the Battery Pennington rail tunnel. To the left is Battery Pennington's plotting and switchboard rooms. (October 2000 – McGovern Collection)

A remaining Panama Mount for a 155-mm mobile gun on the beach at Fort Story. Beach erosion has undermined this mount. (October 2000 – McGovern Collection)

Gun casemate for Battery Ketcham (#120) at Fort Story. This battery is now used for storage. (October 2000 – McGovern Collection)

Battery #227 on Fisherman Island with one of the gun positions in the foreground and the toppled battery commander's station in the background. (October 2000 – McGovern Collection)

Fire control tower located over the second mine casemate at Fort Story. This tower was removed in 2007 when the US Navy stopped using it for R&D activities. (October 2000 – McGovern Collection)

One of the two rare surviving fire control towers on Mockhorn Island, VA. (October 2000 – McGovern Collection)

Gun casemate with protective canopy at Battery Winslow (#122), Fort John Custis, VA (October 2000 – McGovern Collection)

Battery #228 at Fort John Custis, VA has had its entrances and gun positions covered with earth. (October 2000 – McGovern Collection)

Smith Island lighthouse and three World War II fire control steel towers each with three levels for different batteries (two are concrete slab construction and one is steel sheets). (October 2000 – McGovern Collection)

The remains of emplacement No 1 for Antiaircraft Battery No. 1 at Fort Story, VA (October 2000 – McGovern Collection)

Battery Worcester (#224) was the first of the World War II 6-inch emplacement at Fort Story, VA when it was complete in April 1941 (October 2000 – McGovern Collection)

Battery #121 mounted two 16-inch guns when completed in 1943 at Fort Story, VA. (October 2000 – McGovern Colletion)

Cape Henry at Fort Story, VA with both its 1st and 2nd lighthouse. In the background, the U.S. Navy practice amphibious landings. (October 2000 – McGovern Collection).

World War II signal station on the wall of the old Fort Monroe was used as a secondary HECP during the war. (October 2000 – McGovern Collection)

Battery Cramer (#225) was the second of three 6-inch batteries at Fort Story, VA. (October 2000 – McGovern Collection)

Looking north from Old Point Comfort shows the old stone fort, Endicott batteries, and supporting structures at Fort Monroe, VA (October 2000 – McGovern Collection)

Battery #226 was the third of three 6-inch batteries at Fort Story, VA. (October 2000 – McGovern Collection)

The disappearing gun emplacement of Battery Parrott at Fort Monroe, VA is the site of the World War II AMTB Battery #23 and its surviving fixed mount 90mm gun. (October 2000 – McGovern Collection)

The earth protecting the plotting room, battery commander's station, magazine and shell rooms for ATMB Battery #21 at Fort Story, VA has been removed. The fixed gun mounts were located by the concrete ammo storage units between the parking lot and the beach. (October 2000 – McGovern Collection)

This 6-inch Model 1905A2 gun on a shielded barbette carriage M1 was located at Battery #227 on Fisherman Island, VA during World War II. It's now at Battery #123 at Fort Pickens, FL. (October 1994 – McGovern Collection)

Fort Wool at the Rip Raps, VA (October 2000 – McGovern Collection)

Three World War II fire control steel towers each with three levels for different batteries (two are concrete slab construction and one is steel sheets) on Smith Island, VA. (October 2000 – McGovern Collection)

Fire control tower at Parcel D site, located over the second mine casemate at Fort Story. It served Battery Worcester, Battery Cramer, and the nearby minefield. This tower was removed in 2007 when the US Navy stopped using it for R&D activities. (October 2000 – McGovern Collection)

Muzzle of one of the 16-inch howitzer at Battery Pennington, Fort Story, VA. (March 1942 – Library of Congress Collection)

These World War II fire control towers on Mockhorn Island, VA are rare surviving examples of this type of steel towers. (October 2000 – McGovern)

Fort Monroe at Old Point Comfort, VA. (October 2000 – McGovern Collection)

This 6-inch Model 1905A2 gun on a shielded barbette carriage M1 was located at Battery #227 on Fisherman Island, VA during World War II. It's now at Battery #123 at Fort Pickens, FL. (October 1994 – McGovern Collection)

The rear of Battery Cramer (#225) under construction at Fort Story, VA. (February 13, 1942 – Casemate Museum Collection)

Moving a 16-inch gun tube into the gun casemate number 2 at Battery #121 at Fort Story, VA. (September 28, 1941 – Casemate Museum Collection)

Construction of Battery Ketcham (#120) gun casemates and service gallery at Fort Story, VA (January 1942 – Casemate Museum Collection)

One of the shielded barbette carriages at Battery Cramer (#225) at Fort Story, VA being lowered into its emplacement. (March 1943 – Casemate Museum Collection)

Moving a 16-inch gun tube for Battery #121, Fort Story, VA (September 28, 1943 – Casemate Museum Collection)

Preparing for proof firing of a 16-inch gun at Battery Ketcham (#120) at Fort Story, VA. Note that the shield that protects the gun itself has not been yet installed. (October 1942 – Casemate Museum Collection)

U.S. Army Mine Planter underway. Note the special cranes to lift the mines and anchors. (1930's – Still Pictures Collection, NARA)

Late in 1940 the US Navy initiated planning for the establishment of Harbor Entrance Control Posts (HECP). The HECP was a combined intelligence, observation, and communication centre for both the US Army and US Navy to control the movement of shipping. It was first established in the US Weather Bureau building at Fort Story and operated separately from the US Army command post until a new protected harbor defense command post was completed in December 1941. The HECP for the Chesapeake Bay began operation on July 3, 1941. The recently constructed Signal Station at Fort Monroe became a second HECP for the control of shipping entering Hampton Roads and it directed the gate vessel on the anti-submarine gate off Thimble Shoals, and was an adjunct to the HECP at Fort Story.[11] Located below the Signal Station in renovated and modernised casemates, the third front of the old fort became the protected US Army command post for the Chesapeake Bay Sector headquarters and Hampton Roads Groupment. A Joint Operations Center for both the Sector and Naval District was located at the US Naval Operating Base, Norfolk.

World War II comes to the Chesapeake Bay

The first reports of the attack on Pearl Harbor were received on the afternoon of December 7, 1941. The entire command was put on alert status and battle stations were manned. Coast artillery troops were dispatched to guard key infrastructure in the Tidewater area from possible sabotage until the 116th Infantry Regiment, along with a detachment of the 111th Field Artillery, arrived to take over these duties as the Sector's mobile forces. The mission of the mobile force was to observe and patrol the coastline, repel enemy raids or landing attempts, to protect the interior of the sector against attack by airborne troops, and to support the harbor defenses in local

Camouflage over gun casemate number 2 at Battery Ketcham (#120) at Fort Story, VA (1943 – Casemate Museum Collection)

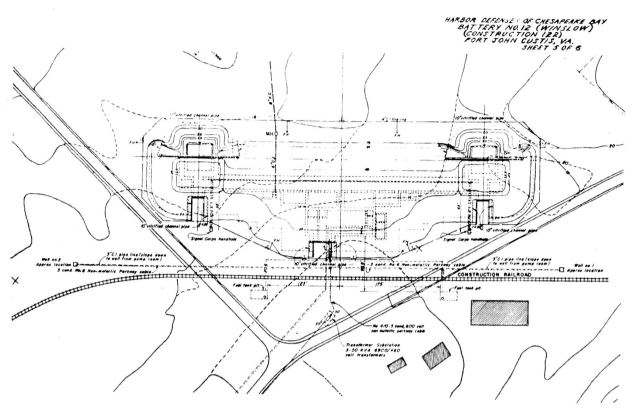

Report of Completed Works – U.S. Corp of Engineers site plan for Battery Winslow (#122), Fort John Custis, VA. (October 1943 – Textural Records Collection, NARA)

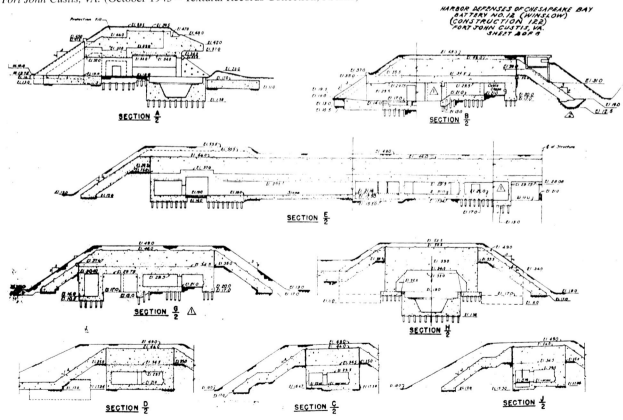

Report of Completed Works – U.S. Corp of Engineers plan for Battery Winslow (#122), Fort John Custis, VA. (October 1943 – Textural Records Collection, NARA)

Battery Commander's station on steel tower for Battery #226 at Fort Story, VA. (March 19, 1943 – Casemate Museum Collection)

World War II signal station on the southeast bastion of the old fort was used as a secondary HECP at Fort Monroe, VA. (April 24, 1942 – Casemate Museum Collection)

defense. On December 10, 1941 orders from First Army activated the Chesapeake Bay Sector. The anti-aircraft defense of the area was also initiated with the 71st Coast Artillery and 74th Coast Artillery regiments who occupied positions covering the Naval Operating Base, Norfolk and Navy Yard in Portsmouth with mobile 3-inch guns, 37-mm weapons, 50-calibre machines guns, and mobile searchlights.

Orders were received on December 8 to initiate the underwater defenses, but this project presented some complications. The materiel was scattered between Fort Monroe and Fort Wool, and the new Little Creek Mine Base had only begun its construction programme that day. By December 31, 1941 nine groups of mines (each group had 19 mines) had been laid despite adverse weather conditions. A US Navy minefield of 365 Mark 6 floating mines was laid by January 17, 1942. Work on the US Army controlled minefield proceeded slowly because of sea conditions, but was completed on March 16, 1942. The Cape-controlled minefields had 22 groups in four lines and were only placed on contact mode if the tactical situation required. Mine operations for the outer fields were conducted from the Little Creek Mine Base while the mines were controlled from a mine casemate at Fort Story (built in 1922) and a mine casemate to be constructed on Fisherman Island. The inner controlled minefield of six groups in two lines was supported from the Fort Monroe mine complex, including a new mine casemate in old casemates of the third front near the East Gate of the old fort. During normal operations and when shipping was entering or leaving, the controlled minefields were kept in the 'safe' mode but were put on 'contact' mode whenever the harbor defense commander decided that the tactical situation required it, at night, or under conditions of poor visibility. There was an opening in the minefields for ships, but there was a great deal of trouble with ships getting off course and striking mines and fouling cables. The situation was finally corrected by using small buoys to show the openings.

On March 1, 1942, the anti-motor torpedo boat net and gate outside Hampton Roads was completed, followed by the York River net on March 8, 1942. The inner minefield was completed and in operation by early April 1942, despite delays caused by the temporary detachment of the Army mine planter *Schofield* to Delaware Bay. The old *Schofield* was the only mine planter available in Chesapeake Bay at that time.

To fill the gap until the new batteries could be complet-

Old Cape Henry Lighthouse and new barrack construction at Fort Story, VA. (January 29, 1941 – Still Picture Collection, NARA)

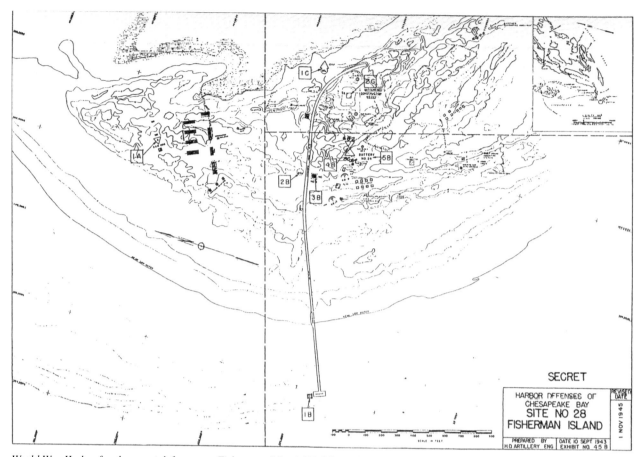
World War II plan for the coast defenses on Fisherman Island, VA (November 1, 1945 – Harbor Defense Project Chesapeake Bay, Annex A)

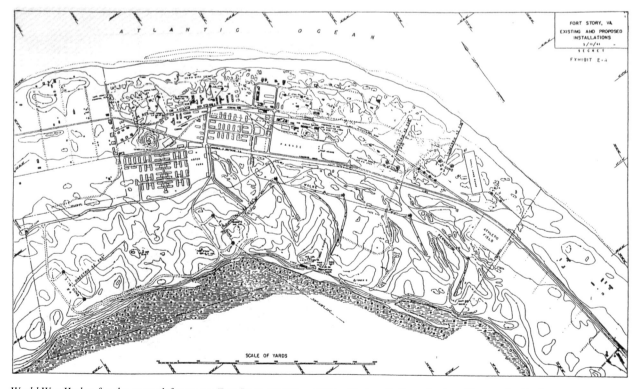
World War II plan for the coast defences on Fort Story, VA (May, 1941 – Harbor Defense Project Chesapeake Bay)

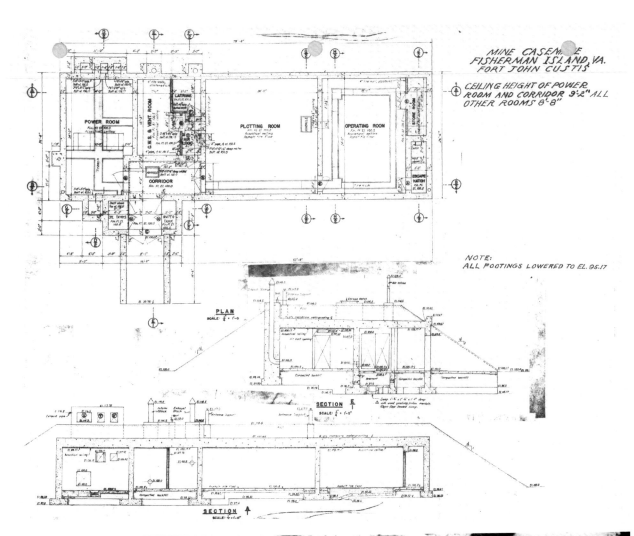

Report of Completed Works – U.S. Corp of Engineers plan for the mine casemate at Fisherman Island, VA. (October 1943 – Textural Records Collection, NARA)

Mine Casemate Number 2 at Fort Story, VA (May 17, 1924 – Still Pictures Collection, NARA)

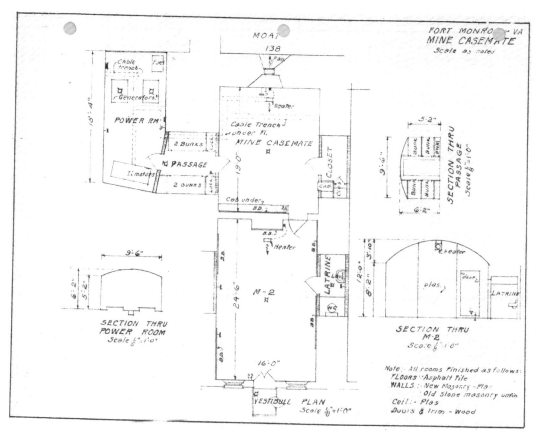

Report of Completed Works – U.S. Corp of Engineers plan for Mine Casemate, Fort Monroe, VA. (October 1942 – Textural Records Collection, NARA)

ed, 8-inch railway guns and 155-mm GPF mobile guns were used for temporary batteries. Two 8-inch railways guns were dispatched from Fort Monroe and arrived at Cape Charles on December 20, 1941. The battle allowance of ammunition, however, did not arrive until December 29, 1941. In August 1942, the 1st Battalion, 52nd Coast Artillery, arrived from Fort Hancock, New Jersey, and replaced these guns with eight more modern M6 railway guns. These guns formed Batteries T8A and T8B. Battery 9T, consisting of two 155-mm guns, was emplaced on the north side of Fort Story, covering the Lynnhaven anchorage and inside entrance to the Capes. Relatively simple and inexpensive platforms, known as Panama Mounts, were used for the 155-mm guns. These guns were mounted on a platform consisting of a curved rail embedded in concrete along which the gun's twin trails could easily be traversed. Similar emplacements for 155-mm guns were constructed on Fisherman Island as well. Even a few 75-mm field guns were used on occasion for temporary batteries. Many of the older permanent batteries were also retained, although at best obsolescent. Battery DeRussy, at Fort Monroe, consisting of three 12-inch disappearing guns, remained in service until November 1943.[12]

While the tactical forces settled in, various changes were made in the armament of the harbor defenses. To adequately cover the examination anchorage in Lynnhaven Roads, located just inside Cape Henry, a two-gun 3-inch rapid fire battery was constructed next to the Fort Story Officers Club, on the west end of the reservation. The guns for the battery were transferred from Battery Henry Lee at Fort Wool. The Examination Battery consisted of a small concrete magazine and two guns pads and was assigned

Planting mines from the U.S. Army Mine Planter General Schofield *and Army Mine Yawl L66 in Chesapeake Bay.* (May 1942 – Still Pictures Collection, NARA)

the Tactical Number 19. After some delays, the battery was ready in late August 1942, allowing the 155-mm battery to be deactivated. The rangefinder was masked by the officers' club building and a depression range finder station was substituted.[13]

The possibility of attack by fast motor torpedo boats posed an unanswered problem at the beginning of the war. As a temporary measure, the old 3-inch rapid fire guns originally intended for minefield protection were used for anti-motor torpedo boat (AMTB) defense. Besides the Examination Battery at Fort Story, two guns from Battery Lee at Fort Wool were transferred to Fisherman Island on the north side of the entrance to the bay. Consisting of a reinforced magazine and two concrete guns pads, this battery, known as Battery No 20, was begun in May 1942 and completed in August 1942 at a cost of over $16,000.[14]

The permanent solution to the AMTB problem came with the 90-mm antiaircraft gun. The first of these batteries was Battery No 21 at Fort Story located slightly west of Battery Worcester. This unique battery was completed on August 2, 1943, at a cost of $35,622, and was used by the US Coast Artillery Board to devise tactics for this type of defense. It looked very similar to a miniature of the new 6-inch batteries, having a large reinforced concrete magazine with a battery commander station on top and the concrete gun pads in front. All subsequent 90-mm batteries had only simple magazines and no built-in commander station. The battery consisted on two fixed 90-mm guns and two mobile 90-mm guns, augmented by mobile 37-mm (later 40-mm) guns. The guns could be

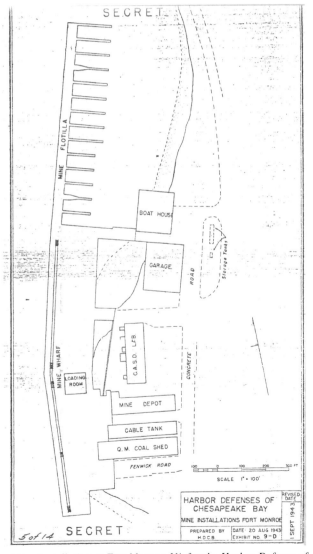

Plan of underwater defences in the Harbor Defense of the Chesapeake Bay, VA (November 1, 1945 – Harbor Defense Project Chesapeake Bay, Annex A)

Mine Installation at Fort Monroe, VA for the Harbor Defense of the Chesapeake Bay, VA (September 1, 1943 – Harbor Defense Project Chesapeake Bay, Annex A)

used for AMTB and anti-aircraft defense and could be radar controlled. Another 90-mm battery, No 22, was begun on April 13, 1943, and completed on December 30, 1943. This battery of the simpler design was also constructed at Fort Story, at a cost of $5,085.[15]

To protect the north side of the mouth of the bay, another 90-mm AMTB Battery, No 24, was built on Fisherman Island between December 1942 and December 1943 at a cost of $6,936. This battery replaced Battery No 20 (mounting 3-inch rapid fire guns), which was removed. The final AMTB battery in Chesapeake Bay was placed at Fort Monroe to cover the entrance to Hampton Roads. In November 1942, General Tilton had recommended that the existing emplacement of Battery Parrott be used for this purpose. The 12-inch disappearing guns that had until this time been used for Coast Artillery School training

An 8-inch Mk VI Mod 3A2 railway gun of the 52nd Coast Artillery emplaced at Fort John Custis, VA. (1942 – Casemate Museum Collection)

Gun Drill on an 8-inch Model 1888 M1A1 on a Model 1918 railway carriage at Fort Monroe, VA. (1943 – Casemate Museum Collection)

Gun drill on a 155-mm Model 1917/18 GPF gun on a 180-degree Panama Mount at Fort Story, VA. (1942 – Casemate Museum Collection)

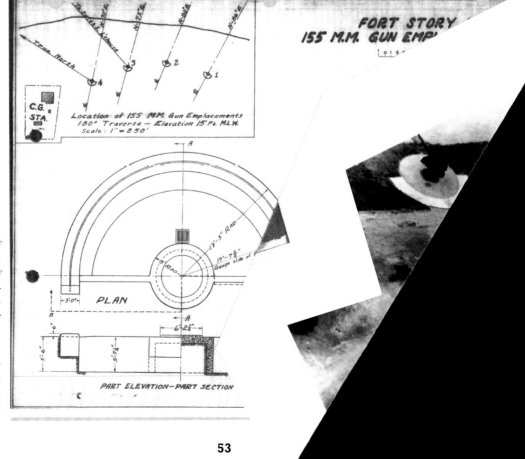

Report of Completed Works – U.S. Corp of Engineers plan for Panama Mounts for 155-mm GPF guns Battery U, Fort Story, VA. (October 1943 – Textural Records Collection, NARA)

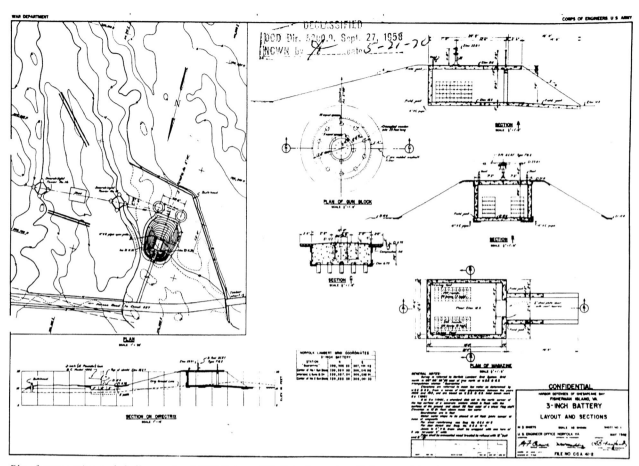

Plan for magazine and shell room for ATMB Battery #20 (3-inch guns) at Fisherman Island, VA. (May 1942 – Textural Records Collection, NARA)

Examination battery with two 3-inch Model 1905 guns on pedestal mounts Model 1902 at Fort Story, VA. (August 1942 – Casemate Museum Collection)

were removed and Battery No 23 was begun in June 1943 and completed in August 1943. The battery used the existing gun pits, with small concrete platforms for the 90-mm fixed guns installed almost up to the parapet level.[16]

Despite the completion of these AMTB batteries, a significant gap still remained in the torpedo boat defenses. The wide entrance to the bay at the Capes prevented the AMTB batteries on Fisherman Island and Fort Story from completely covering the sea area. On 23 November 1942, General Tilton recommended either the construction of an artificial island on the tail of the shallow Middle Ground in the center of the entrance, the construction of a structure similar to the British Maunsell tower, or an anchored hulk as a battery platform. Because of cost, time of construction, and engineering problems, the first two suggestions were not considered. The US Navy agreed to recondition the old gunboat *Annapolis* and to station it at the entrance to the Capes manned by Coast Artillery personnel, but the ship was withdrawn by the US Navy in August 1943 on account of the improved tactical situation. As a result, the problem of the gap in the defenses remained until the end of the war.[17]

The first experimental fire control radar was installed by the US Coast Artillery Board at Fort Story on May 4 1942.

90-mm gun on fixed mount at Battery Parrott, Fort Monroe, VA. (October 2000 – McGovern Collection)

The Plotting Room, Battery Commander's Station, Magazine and Shell Rooms for ATMB Battery #21 at Fort Story, VA while the corner of one of the 90-mm guns can be seen. (August 20, 1943 – Casemate Museum Collection)

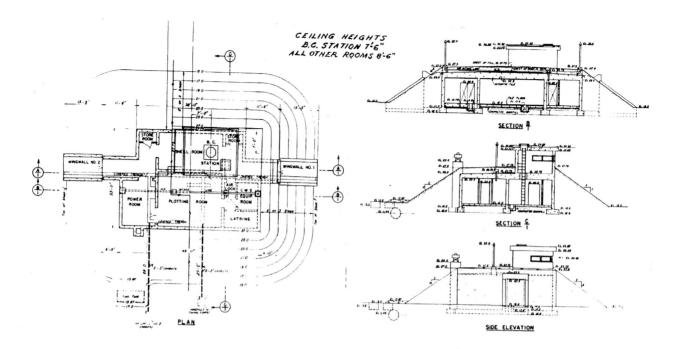

Report of Completed Works – U.S. Corp of Engineers plan for the Plotting Room, Battery Commander's Station, Magazine and Shell Rooms for ATMB Battery #21 at Fort Story, VA. (October 1943 – Textural Records Collection, NARA)

The radar proved a success and was used by one of the 6-inch batteries. But even earlier, on the night of February 16, 1942, the American tanker *E H Blum* approached the Capes in a thick fog. Although known to be friendly, the ship did not answer radio calls. Tracked by radar, she approached the US Army controlled mine field, touched several times, and turned seaward. She entered the US Navy mine field and struck a mine and sank, the Coast Guard eventually rescuing the crew. This was the first time that the harbor defense radar picked up and tracked a vessel in the fog, and the fire control sections were able to predict when she would touch the US Army mine field and exactly where she would contact the US Navy contact mines.

To avoid the problems posed to friendly shipping by the US Navy floating contact mines, the US Army in February 1943 began planting new controlled ground mines (the old controlled mines were a buoyant type that rested only 15 feet below the surface) to replace both the original US Army mines and the US Navy mines. This effort was completed in August 1943. Planting and maintaining these mines required three mine planters, many small boats, and three batteries of coast artillery troops, about 650 men. This was the largest mine project carried out on the East Coast during the war.

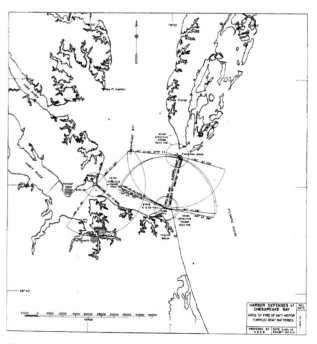

Plan of field of fire for AMTB batteries in the Harbor Defense of the Chesapeake Bay, VA (November 1, 1945 – Harbor Defense Project Chesapeake Bay, Annex A)

In July 1942, the first SCR-582 surveillance radar was installed in the Fort Story command post, followed in November by a second such unit at Fort Monroe. These permitted surveillance of all water areas regardless of

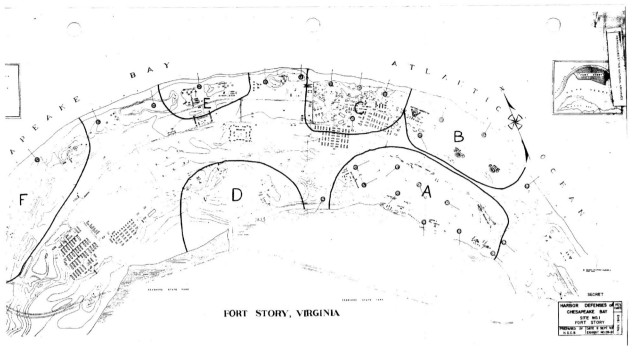

World War II plan for the coast defences on Fort Story, VA (November 1, 1945 – Harbor Defense Project Chesapeake Bay, Annex A)

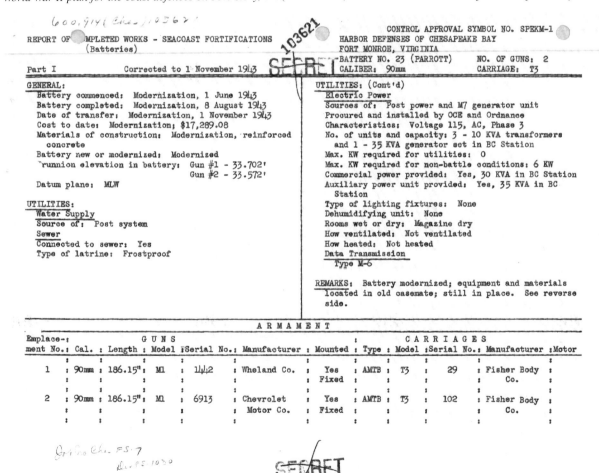

Report of Completed Works – U.S. Corp of Engineers for AMTB Battery #23 at Battery Parrott, Fort Monroe, VA. (November 1943 – Textural Records Collection, NARA)

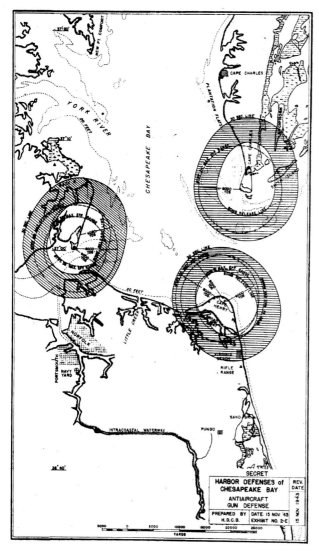

Plan of field of fire for antiaircraft batteries in the Harbor Defense of the Chesapeake Bay, VA (November 1, 1945 – Harbor Defense Project Chesapeake Bay, Annex A)

weather conditions. Any unidentified or doubtful shipping was quickly run down by patrol vessels acting under radar control from one of the HECPs. During November 1942 and early December 1942, a SCR-296 fire control radar was installed in the powder magazine on the right flank of Battery Church at Fort Monroe to support the adjoining Battery Montgomery. Eventually additional SCR-296 sets were installed for Batteries Worcester, Ketcham, Pennington, Walke, Winslow, BCN 227, BCN 121, BCN 228, BCN 226, and Battery Cramer. A SCR-682 seacoast surveillance radar was also placed on Fisherman Island.[18]

The SCR-296 radar was a surface search device developed from the Navy's FD shipboard radar. It operated in the 40 cm frequency at 700 m/c wave length. The antenna was normally enclosed in large cylindrical housing mounted on a high metal tower resembling a small water tower. Despite some important limitations, this radar could provide reliable range on large targets at 40,000 yards, while smaller vessels could only be tracked at ranges of 20,000 yards. The 16-inch guns, however, had a maximum range of 44,900 yards.

The SCR-582 radar operated on a 10.7 cm wavelength at 3,000 m/c. It could track multiple targets and enabled the HECP to function in reduced visibility. The smaller dish antenna was mounted in towers in a similar manner to the SCR-296. It provided results with a maximum range against surface targets of 90,000 yards and an effective range of 35,000 yards. The SCR-682 radar was identical to the SCR-582, but was mounted on three 2½-ton trucks. The antenna could be tilted and operated from a 30 foot tower. It had a maximum range of 240,000 yards with an effective range of 90,000 yards against surface targets.[19]

Work proceeded on the remaining gun batteries around Chesapeake Bay. The Engineers transferred Battery Ketcham following proof firing on February 15, 1943, Battery Construction No 226, and Battery Construction No 121 at Fort Story were transferred as following proof firing on February 15, 1943, and Battery Winslow and Battery Construction No 227 at Fort John Custis to the Coast Artillery Corps on November 12, 1943. This was

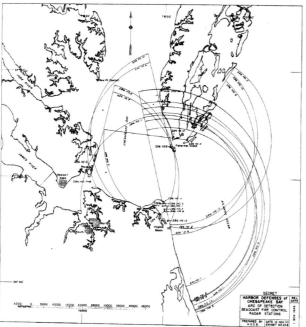

Plan of arc of detection for seacoast fire control radar in the Chesapeake Bay, VA (November 1, 1945 – Harbor Defense Project Chesapeake Bay, Annex A)

followed on November 23, 1943 by Battery Cramer at Fort Story, which had been proof fired in November 1942. The 16-inch Mk II guns and carriages for Battery Ketcham had arrived in May 1942, but the gun shields were still waiting installation in February 1944 because of the settling of the foundation of Gun No 1. The guns and carriages of Battery Winslow did not arrive until August 1943 and for Battery Construction No 121 the following month. Problems again delayed installing shields at Battery Winslow. Battery Ketcham cost $1,553,992, Battery Construction No 121 $1,881,850, and Battery Winslow $1,554,866. The 16-inch howitzers of Battery Pennington (split into two batteries, Pennington and Walke, for administrative purposes in 1941), were not given concrete and steel casemates for overhead protection but instead each gun was provided with a splinter-proof shield to protect the gun.

While the 6-inch batteries in design were identical, the guns differed slightly. Battery Cramer had two M1903A2 guns, Battery Construction No 226 two of the newer T2 guns, and Battery Construction No 227 two M1905A2 guns. The completed batteries cost $175,872, $234,602, and $271,352, respectively. The cost of Battery Construction No 227 was so high because of the isolation and difficulty of access of Fisherman Island off the tip of Cape Charles. Two more 6-inch batteries were never completed. Although the emplacements were finished, guns were never mounted at Battery Construction No 228 on Cape Charles and Battery Gates at Fort Wool due to the diversion of gun manufacturing to field artillery late in the war.[20] During this time Fort Story had grown in size to accommodate all the new construction so that the reservation now contained 1,393 acres. Table III contains a listing of batteries that actually existed at Fort John Custis (and its sub-post on Fisherman Island), at Fort Story, and added at Forts Monroe and Wool during the World War II period:

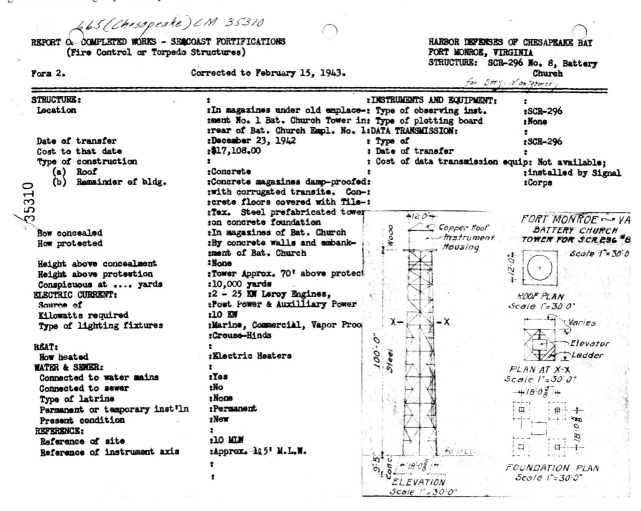

Report of Completed Works – U.S. Corp of Engineers for the SCR-296 radar tower at Fort Monroe, VA. (February 1943 – Textural Records Collection, NARA)

Construction of Battery Cramer (#225), Fort Story, VA nearing completion with one of its 6-inch shielded barbette guns can be seen to the right. (October 28, 1942 – Casemate Museum Collection)

An 8-inch Mk VI Mod 3A2 railway gun assigned to the 52nd Coast Artillery in its firing position at Fort John Custis, VA. (1942 – Casemate Museum Collection)

TABLE III
FORT JOHN CUSTIS

Battery name	# of guns	calibre	carriage type	service years	status	notes
Winslow (#122)	2	16"	CBC	1943-1948		
T8A and T8B	8	8"	RY	1942-1943		
#228	2	6"	SBC	1943-NC	Not completed	Emplacement buried

Fisherman Island

#227	2	6"	SBC	1943-1965	guns to Smithsonian, Power equip. still in place	
unnamed	4	5"	P	1917-1919	2-5"/2-6"?	
Lee (AMTB #20)	2	3"	P	1942-1944	guns from Lee, Ft. Wool, partially buried	
AMTB #24	2	90 mm	F	1943-1946		
unnamed	4?	155 mm	PM	1941-1943		

FORT STORY

Battery name	# of guns	calibre	carriage type	service years	status	notes
Pennington	2	16"	LRH	1922-1947	original name for all 4 guns	
Walke	2	16"	LRH	1922-1947	named as separate battery in 1941, empls. covered	
Ketcham (#120)	2	16"	CBC	1943-1948		
#121	2	16"	CBC	1943-1948		
Worcester (#224)	2	6"	P	1942-1947	prototype for the WW II 6-in construction	
Cramer (#225)	2	6"	SBC	1943-1949		
#226	2	6"	SBC	1943-1949		
unnamed	2	6"	P	1917-1919	broken up, in surf	
unnamed	2	5"	P	1917-1919	broken up, in surf	
Exam (AMTB #19)	2	3"	P	1942-1945	guns from Irwin, Ft. Monroe, buried	
AMTB #21	2	90 mm	F	1942-1948	buried	
AMTB #22	2	90 mm	F	1942-1948	awash	
unnamed	4?	155 mm	PM	1931-1943	awash	
unnamed	4?	155 mm	PM	1941-1943		

FORT MONROE & FORT WOOL

Battery name	# of guns	calibre	carriage type	service years	status	notes
AMTB #23	2	90 mm	F	1943-1946	Built in Bty Parrott's emplacement at Ft. Monroe	
Gates (#229)	2	6"	SBC	1944-NC	Built on top disappearing emplacement	

KEY: F – Fixed Mount   PM – Panama Mount   LRH – Long Range Howitzer   P – Pedestal   RY – Railway
CBC – Casemated Barbette   SBC – Shielded Barbette

The U-Boat Threat

The high point of the German submarine offensive came during the first four months of 1942. During that period, 82 ships were sunk off the American Mid-Atlantic coast. While the construction and arming of the new batteries proceeded at what appeared to General Tilton to be a ponderous pace, the war came to the Chesapeake Bay area. On January 17, an American tanker was sent to the bottom by a German submarine to open a campaign that cost many more ships. The Chesapeake Bay Sector had available in the early months of the war the 65th Observation Group at Langley Field in Hampton, Virginia, to patrol the offshore waters. Navy strength was at first somewhat limited, but on April 14, the USS *Roper*, an old four stacker destroyer, sank the *U-85* off Oregon Inlet, North Carolina. By arrangement with the Sector, the recovered bodies of the crew were buried in the Hampton National Cemetery. A coastal blackout was imposed, which caused continuing problems for the Sector forces in its enforcement.

The war became very real to the defenses of Chesapeake Bay on June 15. A northbound American

Plan of Fort John Custis, VA in the Harbor Defense of the Chesapeake Bay, VA (November 1, 1945 – Harbor Defense Project Chesapeake Bay, Annex A)

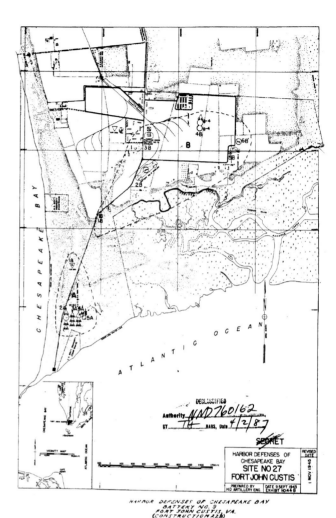

tanker, the *R C Tuttle*, suddenly exploded and was set on fire. The batteries at Fort Story immediately went on alert and planes from Langley were sent to the area. About half an hour later the *Esso Augusta*, another American tanker, was struck. About that time the US Navy destroyer USS *Bainbridge* (DD 246) was damaged by another explosion. The convoy and the harbor defenses could find no evi-

Photo of HMS Kingston Ceylonite *and SS* Tiger *– both ship sunk by U-boats off Cape Henry* (Photos from *Fort Story and Cape Henry* by Fielding Lewis Tyler – 2005 Arcadia Publishing)

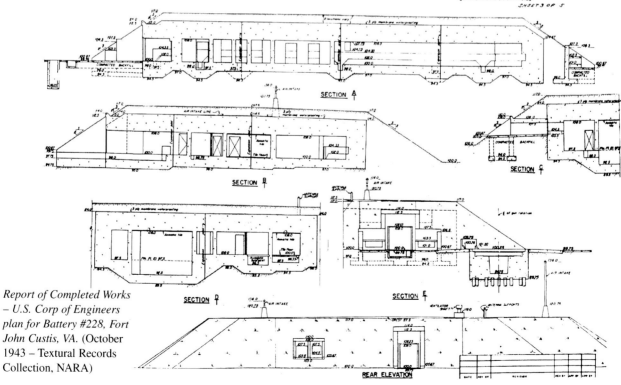

Report of Completed Works – U.S. Corp of Engineers plan for Battery #228, Fort John Custis, VA. (October 1943 – Textural Records Collection, NARA)

Report of Completed Works – U.S. Corp of Engineers layout for Battery #228, Fort John Custis, VA. (October 1943 – Textural Records Collection, NARA)

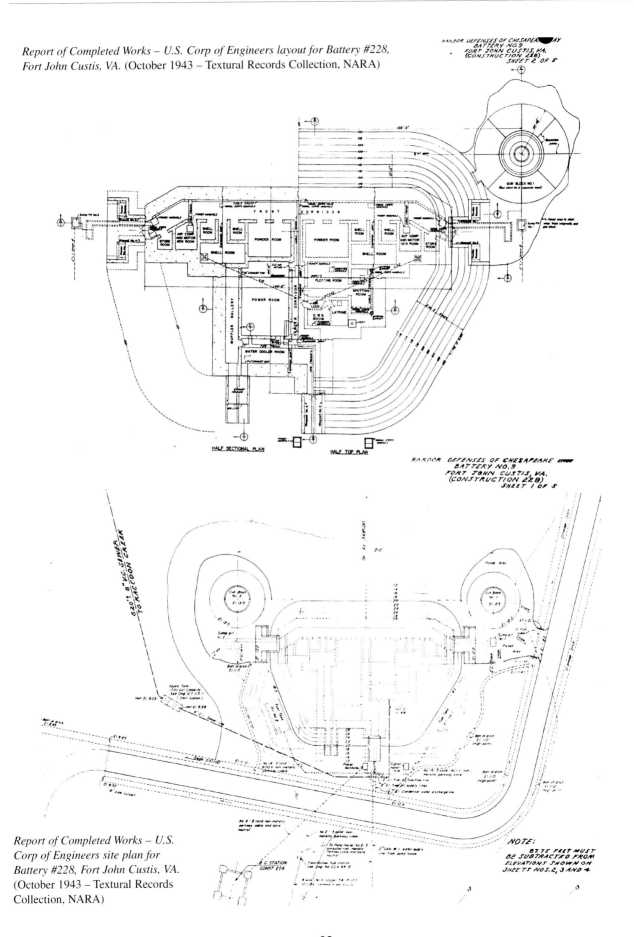

Report of Completed Works – U.S. Corp of Engineers site plan for Battery #228, Fort John Custis, VA. (October 1943 – Textural Records Collection, NARA)

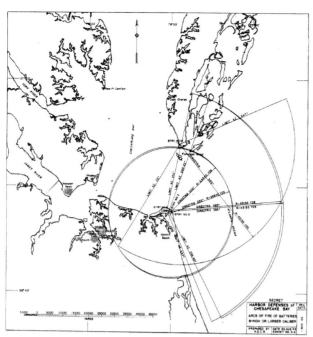

Plan of field of fire for batteries with guns greater than 8-inch in size for the Harbor Defense of the Chesapeake Bay, VA (November 1, 1945 – Harbor Defense Project Chesapeake Bay, Annex A)

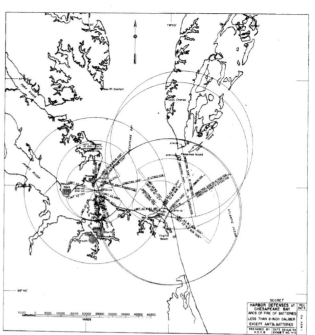

Plan of field of fire for batteries with guns less than 6-inch in size for the Harbor Defense of the Chesapeake Bay, VA (November 1, 1945 – Harbor Defense Project Chesapeake Bay, Annex A)

dence of a submarine. Three hours later the British anti-submarine trawler HMS *Kingston Ceylonite* (FY214), part of the convoy escort (and at the time on temporary loan to the US Navy), exploded and sank with the loss of 18 out of 32 hands. The *Tuttle* managed to limp into port despite its damage. The defenses went off general alert at midnight, but two days later the American collier *Santore* was sunk in the same area. A sweep of the channel resulted in the explosion of 13 mines.

The attack took place within the range of the heavy armament at Fort Story and of a 155-mm battery in position at Camp Pendleton (a Coast Artillery Training Center) in Virginia Beach. There had been no reports of submarine contact in the mined area and it was concluded that a submarine had come in under cover of darkness or poor visibility and had laid mines some time before. This was confirmed a month later when *U-701* was sunk off Cape Hatteras by an Army Air Corps A-29 medium attack bomber out of Cherry Point, North Carolina. The seven survivors of the crew, including the captain, were picked up and spent the rest of the war as prisoners. The *U-701* had approached Chesapeake Bay on the night of June 12 and was startled to find the target clearly illuminated. The submarine was on the surface, because the water was too shallow to submerge. Fifteen mines were successfully laid and set to activate 60 hours after release.[21]

The War moves away from Chesapeake Bay

Even as the permanent defenses of Chesapeake Bay neared completion, steps began to greatly reduce the commitment of resources to harbor defense. Before the start of the war, the US War Department had planned to reduce the number of troops manning harbor defenses as soon as the military situation permitted. As a result, on November 1, 1943, the category of defense of the Eastern Defense Command was reduced to a coastal frontier probably free from attack, but which, for political reasons, must provide nominal defense to repel raids by submarines, surface ships, or isolated raids by aircraft.

At the beginning of the war, there were 11,263 troops assigned to the Chesapeake Bay Sector. This force grew to 15,965 by September 1943. With the start of the drawdown, the troop strength dropped to 13,293 by December 1943 and to 9,000 in March 1944. The Chesapeake Bay Sector was formally inactivated on March 1, 1944. All of the sector obligations in Hampton Roads were absorbed by the Harbor Defenses of Chesapeake Bay, again commanded by General Tilton, whose headquarters moved from Fort Story back to Fort Monroe. The Temporary Harbor Defenses of Beaufort Inlet and the mobile force passed to the control of a new Southeastern Sector.

A reorganization of the units assigned to the Harbor Defenses of Chesapeake Bay soon followed in early

March 1944, resulting in the headquarters and headquarters batteries of the 1st, 2nd, and 3rd Battalions of the 2nd Coast Artillery, along with Battery N, less the searchlight platoon, being transferred to Camp Rucker, Alabama. In September 1943, the 246th Coast Artillery was disbanded and the remaining elements of the 2nd Coast Artillery were reorganized into the 2nd Coast Artillery Battalion and 175th Coast Artillery Battalion. A further reorganization and reduction in March 1945 resulted in the deactivation of the 175th Coast Artillery Battalion and all but two batteries of the 2nd Coast Artillery Battalion. Batteries A to F, Harbor Defenses of Chesapeake Bay, manned the defenses until the end of the war. Troop strength dropped to about 2,000.[22]

The HECPs continued operations, and the mine defenses were retained intact. The armament on alert was reduced to one 6-inch battery and one AMTB battery at Fort Story, the same at Fisherman Island, and the ATMB battery at Fort Monroe. The remaining armament was placed on full maintenance status with reduced personnel. Submarine contacts continued in the area and the last attack occurred on April 23, 1945.

As the threat of enemy attacks to the Chesapeake Bay area dissipated in 1945, defense measures were gradually reduced and in March 1945 orders were received to start taking up the controlled minefield. This was a major operation, made more difficult by the transfer in December 1944 of the two large, modern mine planters, the *Knox* and the *Murray*, to the US Navy for use in the Pacific. As a result, only the old mine planter *Schofield* and other work boats that could be borrowed were assigned to pick up the minefields. By August 1945, over 125,000 pounds of TNT was on hand from recovered mines and 15 groups of mines had yet to be recovered. Orders were finally received to dispose of the TNT at sea and remaining mines to be blown up where they were planted.

The end of the war brought a quick end to the extensive defenses which had been constructed in the Chesapeake Bay area. After the German surrender on May 8, 1945, the alert status was further reduced and finally ended with the Japanese surrender on August 14, 1945. The modernisation of the harbor defenses had been practically completed, with only a few batteries missing

HARBOR DEFENSES OF CHESAPEAKE BAY
TABULATION OF SEACOAST ARMAMENT REQUIRED BY BASIC PROJECT

TACTICAL NUMBER	NAME OF BATTERY	NO. OF GUNS	CALIBER AND MODEL OF GUNS	MODEL OF MOUNT	RANGE FOR MAX. ELEVATION	LOCATION BY FORTS	EXISTING OR PROJECTED	ARMAMENT EMPLACED OR NOT	STATUS ON COMPLN. RETND OR ABANDND	EXHIBIT NUMBER	
1	KETCHAM	2	16" Gun Navy Mk II M1	M4	45,155 yds	Fort Story	Existing	Emplaced	Retained	2-B	(2)
2	PENNINGTON	2	16" Howitzer M 1920	M 1920	24,540 yds	Fort Story	Existing	Emplaced	Retained	3-B	①
3	WALKER	2	16" Howitzer M 1920	M 1920	24,540 yds	Fort Story	Existing	Emplaced	Retained	4-B	①
4	CONST. NO. 121	2	16" Gun Navy Mk II M1	M4	45,155 yds	Fort Story	Existing	Emplaced	Retained	5-B	(2)
5	CRAMER	2	6" Gun M 1905 A2	M2	27,520 yds	Fort Story	Existing	Emplaced	Retained	6-B	
6	WORCESTER	2	6" Gun M 1900	M 1900	19,600 yds	Fort Story	Existing	Emplaced	Retained	7-B	①
7	MINES	-	- - -	-	- -	Fort Story Casemate	Existing	- -	Retained	- -	
8	MINES	-	- - -	-	- -	Fisherman Island Casemate	Existing	- -	Retained	- -	
9	CONST. NO. 225	2	6" Gun M1	M4	27,520 yds	Fort John Custis	Existing	Emplaced	Retained	8-B	①
10	CONST. NO. 226	2	6" Gun M1	M4	27,520 yds	Fort Story	Existing	Emplaced	Retained	9-B	
11	CONST. NO. 227	2	6" Gun M 1905 A2	M1	27,520 yds	(Fisherman Island) Fort John Custis	Existing	Emplaced	Retained	10-B	
12	WINSLOW	2	16" Navy Mk II M1	M4	45,155 yds	Fort John Custis	Existing	Emplaced	Retained	11-B	(2)
13	CONST. NO. 229 (GATES)	2	6" Gun M1	M4	27,520 yds	Fort Wool	Existing	Emplaced	Retained	12-B	①
14	HINDMAN	2	6" Gun M 1903 M1	M1903	11,800 yds	Fort Wool	Existing	Emplaced	Retained	13-B	
15	MINES	-	- - -	-	- -	Fort Monroe Casemate	Existing	- -	Retained	- -	
16	LEE	4	3" Gun M 1902 M1	M1902	11,360 yds	Fort Wool	Existing	Emplaced	Retained	14-B	
17	MONTGOMERY	2	6" Gun M 1900	M 1900	16,200 yds	Fort Monroe	Existing	Emplaced	Retained	15-B	①
18	NOT ASSIGNED TO EXISTING ARMAMENT										
19	EXAMINATION BTRY	2	3" Gun M 1902 M1	M1902	10,950 yds	Fort Story	Existing	Emplaced	Retained	16-B	
20	NOT ASSIGNED TO EXISTING ARMAMENT										
21	AMTB NO. 21	4	90mm Gun AA M1	2-T5 2-M1 A1	7,500 yds *	Fort Story	Existing	Emplaced	Retained	17-B	
		2	40mm Gun M1	Mobile M2 A1	4,300 yds						
22	AMTB NO. 22	4	90mm Gun AA M1	2-T5 2-M1 A1	7,500 yds *	Fort Story	Existing	Emplaced	Retained	18-B	
		2	40mm Gun M1	Mobile M2A1	4,300 yds						
23	AMTB NO. 23	4	90mm Gun AA M1	2-T5 2-M1 A1	7,500 yds *	Fort Monroe	Existing	Emplaced	Retained	19-B	
		2	40mm Gun M1	Mobile M2 A1	4,300 yds						
24	AMTB NO. 24	4	90mm Gun AA M1	2-T5 2-M1 A1	7,500 yds *	(Fisherman Island) Fort John Custis	Existing	Emplaced	Retained	20-B	
		2	40mm Gun M1	Mobile M2 A1	4,300 yds						

SECRET   REVISED 1 NOV. 45   EXHIBIT 2-A

* – Maximum effective range against motor torpedo boats is 7,500 yds; firing table maximum range is 19,560 yds.   625 Fort Monroe—45

Table of seacoast armament for basic project in the Harbor Defense of the Chesapeake Bay, VA (November 1, 1945 – Harbor Defense Project Chesapeake Bay, Annex A)

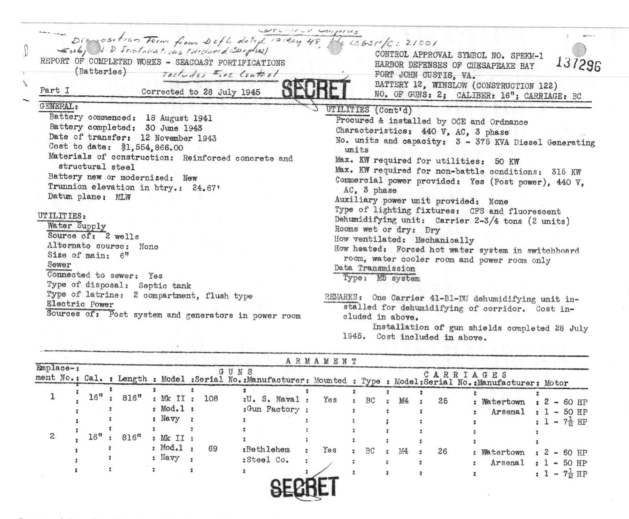

Report of Completed Works – U.S. Corp of Engineers plan for the mine casemate at Fisherman Island, VA. (October 1943 – Textural Records Collection, NARA)

their guns or key fire control equipment, such as gun data computers. Several of the new batteries held practices, such as Battery Ketcham at Fort Story which fired 20 rounds on November 27, 1945. In May 1946, the headquarters of the US Army Ground Forces moved to Fort Monroe forcing the relocation of the Harbor Defenses of Chesapeake Bay to Fort Story. At the same time the Coast Artillery School which had operated at Fort Monroe in various forms since 1824 was moved to Fort Winfield Scott in San Francisco, California. June 14, 1946 saw General Tilton relieved of command of the Chesapeake Bay defenses after serving in this role since 1940.

In the summer of 1946 the US War Department Seacoast Defense Armament Board was created, chaired by General Tilton, to review the existing harbor defenses of the United States and recommended what should be retained. The board recommended that harbor defenses should be retained but reduced to minefields and submarine mine facilities, modern 6-inch guns covering minefields, modern 16-inch guns, associated fire control stations, and the minimum of buildings to support these retained facilities. The rapid reduction of the armed forces, money constraints, and an assessment of defensive needs based on wartime experience, however, soon resulted in the end of the fixed harbor defenses and the US Coast Artillery Corps. The final guns were removed from Chesapeake Bay by late 1949 (except for two 6-inch guns and two 90mm guns but they were abandoned in place) and the Harbor Defenses of Chesapeake Bay was deactivated on January 1, 1950.[23]

Aftermath

Since 1950 many of structures and sites of these former defenses have slowly disappeared through reuse, commercial development, and exposure to nature. Given the large US military presence in the area some sites were converted to other military uses, such as storage, workshops, research and development laboratories, and communication stations. Surplus properties were transferred to other governmental agencies for use as parks and wildlife refuges. Smaller parcels were returned to their former owners or sold in auctions to private interests. Most of the wood-framed structures have been destroyed while most of the steel towers (fire control, radar, or searchlight) have been removed. The concrete structures have survived except where beach erosion has claimed the site, especially for the smaller calibre batteries, while some emplacements have been buried.

The primary coast defense sites remain. Fort John Custis was used by the US Air Force for many years as a tracking station, but today is part of the eastern shore of Virginia National Wildlife Refuge. Battery Winslow is open to visitors, while Battery No 228 is buried. The fort's buildings have been removed. The nearby Fisherman Island Military Reservation is now the Fisherman Island National Wildlife Refuge and is off limits to visitors. All buildings have been removed and towers toppled. Battery No 227 retained its two 6-inch shielded barbette guns until 1965 and AMTB Battery No 24 retained its two fixed mount 90-mm gun mounts until 1976 when they were moved. The 6-inch guns are now located at Battery No 234 at Fort Pickens, Florida, while one 90-mm gun is at Battery Parrott at Fort Monroe and the other at Fort MacArthur Military Museum in San Pedro, California. Battery No 227 does retain its three motor generators in its power room although in a derelict condition. Fort Story remains an active military post serving a variety of roles for the US Army, Navy and Marines. Batteries Pennington and Walke are abandoned and their supporting buildings are used for storage. Batteries No 120 and No 121 have been stripped inside and have been reused over the years by several tenants, ranging from a Nike missile battery to a US Navy SEAL unit. The three 6-inch batteries (Nos 224, 225, and 226) have also gone through modifications to be converted into research and development facilities and communication centres. Today they are primarily used for storage. The smaller batteries with the 155-mm, 90-mm and 3-inch guns have been greatly affected by beach erosion so that they are now awash or broken up in the surf. The parcels of land used for searchlights and fire control down the Virginia coast have for the most part been returned to private use.

Fort Wool has been turned into a Hampton city park with a seasonal ferry service. Battery No 229 remains along with one of the few still-standing battery commander's stations located on a steel tower. Fort Monroe is still a US Army post but is scheduled to close in 2011. After World War II the fort's coast artillery role was phased out and it became the headquarters for the US Army ground forces in the Continental USA. That role has evolved over the years to the headquarters for the US Army's training command. The old fort and about half of the Endicott Period batteries survive today. The World War II additions of the mine casemate, harbor defense command post, AMTB Battery No 23, and signal station still remain. The US Naval bases and important shipyards remain in Norfolk and Hampton, but the defense of these important military sites now relies upon warplanes from several military airfield in the area and naval ships themselves. The long history of the coastal defenses of the Chesapeake Bay is reduced to concrete structures and memories of the men that manned these defenses.

Primary Sources

1. Richard P Weinert Jr and Robert Arthur, *Defender of the Chesapeake: The Story of Fort Monroe* (Shippensburg, PA, White Mane Publishing Co, Inc, 1989).
2. Stetson Conn, Rose E Engelman, and Byron Fairchild, *Guarding the United States and Its Outposts* (Washington, Department of the Army, 1964).
3. Harbor Defense Project Chesapeake Bay, Annex A, Supplement to the Harbor Defense Project, Harbor Defenses of Chesapeake Bay (Fort Monroe, VA, US Army, November 1, 1945).
4. 1st Lt. William M Bronk, *A History of the Eastern Defense Command* (New York, 1945).
5. Brig Gen Rollin L Tilton, *History of the Chesapeake Bay Sector* (Fort Monroe, 1945).
6. Report of Completed Work (RWC), Battery Worcester, March 21, 1944, Record Group 77, Records of the Corps of Engineers, National Archives.
7. Fielding Lewis Tyler, *Fort Story and Cape Henry* (Charleston, SC, Arcadia Publishing Co. Inc. 2005).
8. Coast Defense Study Group, Conference Notes for the 17th Annual Conference of the CDSG to the Harbor Defense of Chesapeake Bay (Bel Air, MD, CDSG, 2000).
9. Glen Williford, 'Middle Ground of the Chesapeake Bay – An Almost Fortress' *Coast Defense Journal*, CDSG (November 2000) pp 39-47.

10. Robert Zink, 'The Forts of "Wherever" – James River and Norfolk – Hampton Roads – Chesapeake Bay Defenses' *Coast Defense Study Group News* (November 1991) pp 48-54.

Notes

1. For the evolution and history of the armament at Fort Monroe, see Richard P Weinert, Jr and Robert Arthur, *Defender of the Chesapeake: The Story of Fort Monroe* (Shippensburg, Pa, White Mane Publishing Co, Inc, 1989). Information about Fort Wool may be found in Richard P Weinert, Jr, 'Saga of Old Fort Wool,' *Periodical*, VIII (Winter, 1976-77) pp 3-13.
2. Harbor Defense Project Chesapeake Bay, Annex A, Seacoast Guns, para 1a, NA.
3. 1st Lt. William M Bronk, *A History of the Eastern Defense Command* (New York, 1945), p 18; Brig Gen Rollin L Tilton, *History of the Chesapeake Bay Sector* (Fort Monroe, 1945), p 7.
4. Stetson Conn, Rose E Engelman, and Byron Fairchild, *Guarding the United States and Its Outposts* (Washington, Department of the Army, 1964), pp 47-49; History of the Eastern Defense Command, pp 22-23.
5. Emanuel Raymond Lewis, *Seacoast Fortifications of the United States: An Introductory History* (Washington: Smithsonian Institution Press, 1970), pp 115-118.
6. Annex A, Seacoast Guns, pp 2-3. *History of the Chesapeake Bay Sector*, p 9.
7. Report of Completed Work (RWC), Battery Worcester, March 21, 1944, Record Group 77, Records of the Corps of Engineers, National Archives. The battery was named in honor of Col. Philip Worcester by GO No 5, War Department, January 20, 1942.
8. *History of the Chesapeake Bay Sector*; *History of the Harbor Defenses of Chesapeake Bay*.
9. Journals of Brig Gen Rollin L Tilton, Vol I, pp 251, 252, 257. Interview, Col Harold Broudy, October 13, 1981. Interview, Brig Gen Rollin L. Tilton, December 14, 1974. The daily journals kept by General Tilton are in the collection of the Casemate Museum, Fort Monroe. RCWs, Battery Worcester and Battery Ketcham, March 2, 1944. Battery Construction No 120 was named Battery Ketcham in honor of Brig Gen Daniel Ketcham by GO No 7, War Department, January 24, 1942. Battery Construction No 122 was subsequently named Battery Winslow in honor of Brig Gen E. Eveleth Winslow by GO No 9, War Department, February 5, 1942.
10. *History of the Chesapeake Bay Sector*, p 10; History of the Harbor Defenses of Chesapeake Bay, p 3.
11. *History of the Chesapeake Sector*, pp 13-14.
12. Ibid., pp 17-18, 20, 28, 29; *History of Eastern Defense Command*, pp 24-25; Lewis, Seacoast Fortifications, p 108.
13. Tilton Journals, Vol 1, pp 54, 122, 140, 156.
14. RCW, Battery No 20, January 25, 1944, RG 77.
15. History of Eastern Defense Command, p 25. RCWs, Battery No 21, August 1, 1945, and Battery No 22, December 30, 1943, RG 77.
16. RCW, Battery 24, 12 February 1944, RG 77. *History of the Eastern Defense Command*, p 5. Tilton Journals, Vol 2, p 33. The AMTB batteries became operational on the following dates: No 21, April 6, 1943; No 23, September 15, 1943; No 22, September 22, 1943; and No 24, November 9, 1943. History of the Chesapeake Bay Sector, p 56.
17. *History of the Chesapeake Bay Sector*, p 45.
18. Ibid., pp 32-33, 45-46, 57. Fort Monroe Fort Record Book. Harbor Defenses of Chesapeake Bay, Radar Equipment, Other Than Antiaircraft, November 1, 1945.
19. Danny R Malone, 'Seacoast Armament Radar 1938-46,' Coast Defense Study Group News, 3 (November 1989) pp 1-8.
20. RCWs, Battery Ketchum, Battery Construction No 121, Battery Winslow, Battery Construction No 226, Battery Construction No 227, and Battery Cramer, *History of Chesapeake Bay Sector*, p 56; Tilton Journals, Vol 4, p2.
21. *History of Chesapeake Bay Sector*, pp 30-34, 41-42; articles in the Norfolk Ledger-Star, July 7 and 8, 1982.
22. *History of Chesapeake Bay Sector*, pp 16,54,70, 75; *History of the Harbor Defenses of Chesapeake Bay*, p 4; GO No 4, HDCB, February 29, 1944; SO No 13, Southeastern Sector, September 19, 1944, GO No 3, Southeastern Sector, March 29, 1945.
23. Weinert and Arthur, 'Defender of the Chesapeake', pp 283-284; Richard P Weinert, Jr, 'So the Coast Artillery is Gone – But Not Forgotten,' *Periodical*, X (Fall 1978), pp 20-23.